JUBILEE FOR RENEGADES

jubilee
for re[illegible]

POEMS 1976 - 1980

Truths are illusions which one has forgotten are illusions.
Friedrich Nietzsche

THE DOLMEN PRESS

JUBILEE FOR RENEGADES is designed by Liam Miller, typeset in IBM Journal Roman and printed in the Republic of Ireland by Patternprint Limited for the publishers, The Dolmen Press, Mountrath, Portlaoise, Ireland.

Publication of this book was assisted by a grant from An Comhairle Ealaion (The Arts Council).

First Published 1982

British Library Cataloguing in Publication Data

Maxton, Hugh
Jubilee for Renegades
I. Title
821'.914

ISBN 0 85105 392 0

CONTENTS

I

II

III

IV

ACKNOWLEDGEMENTS

Acknowledgements are due to the editors of the following magazines, in which some of these poems first appeared: *Broadsheet, Chapman, Cyphers, The Green River Review, The Honest Ulsterman, Irish University Review, New Irish Writing, Stand, The Urbane Gorilla.*

"Survivors of Pavilion" was published in 1980 in *The Green River Review:* early versions of some parts of the poem had previously appeared in *Ariel, The Malahat Review, Transatlantic Review.*

"From the German of Johannes Bobrowski" is the result of an extended collaboration with Dennis Tate.

I

EBLANA

i

Then the cedars and other
Various conifers
Grew in motionless swirls
Of resin and air
Round the littoral.

It was the point before
Nature (which had been ours)
Retired landwards.

How the bay stood
Unimaginable,
Light gripped
Each separate essence.

Mes vagues.

ii

My native place.

Great fragments
Drifting in unison,
The harness
Of drowned gods,

Computable
Shadows of a dream.

Where the sea turns
Inward we found
A virgin,
A stooped muse

Persecuted or diligent,
Various.

iii

A gathering of women at nightfall,
An insurgent class,

Many needs graciously unattainable.

Empty mouth of the annalist, such forms,
Plump arse of the revenant housewife.

My tongue is a shadow in your mouth,
A map cast aside on familiar land.

iv

We fell on the lower slopes
On scribes of bog,

For the site of this dream
Eblana.

To reach here
We crossed nothing.

It was a great place to live off!

v

Capital village
Open labyrinth,

Here the statues
Are daubed with excrement.

She spoke, loudly,
Of our oblique relations,

Her fillet of kissed hair
Crimped in thought.

Annal-keeper
Muse
Betrayed daughter.

Empty all these words, empty
As a cup after drinking.

vi

The self is a journey:
Have I not spoken
Bearing this privacy.

Many streets
Under the one sun,
No amazement

No shock at her limbs.
Multitudinous
Muse never meeting

Yet succeed in me,
Tides of desolation
And thanksgiving.

vii

A white wall
Seals your garden.

A city without trees
Is a woman without breasts.

I am happiest away from you
For your prospect delights me.

My love your streets
Echo in my absence.

Exile from your body
Is silence.

Whenever I see you I need you
The converse is not true.

Your white breast
Seals my mouth.

viii

Her eyes, her hair,
Her lips, her gait,
Her voice . . .

I rue the urinous walls,
Our midden of husks.
After the long seas

We ate under siege
Our own elements
And took wine.

I rue such
Infeasible
Secure pleasure.

Perfection is a means
Elsewhere. Not startled
When an otter plunged

In Lake Belvedere
She circled the water,
Plumed, reconciled, alone.

I had touched her head,
The dusk of her eyes
In lustful sympathy.

Now while she spake
She was doing her part
Of this fulfilment.

ix

By the margin of the ocean
Salt sews our appearances

In daily rhythms. Eggs
Cook under the embers.

The boat waits
Its own wharf.

Imminent headlands recede
By the motion of hands.

They are not to be thought away.
From barbarous pasture

And courts of criminal
Charm, Eblana comes

To build a city of water,
Embody later origins.

BEAUMARIS

Tamarisk by Beau Maris,
Water under the tower calm and reflective,
The tower ruined and complete.
How it was. A king labouring
Beyond need in a subject land.

The roots hold in the new soil.
Fascilici in pink or blue
Lighten the air. The castle walls
Hold nothing but heat and guests.
Separate muses parade on the ramparts.

We have met there, above the clean door,
And the restored wood replacing no wood.
Content – that was your term – content;
Across the channel snow covered a cross
Cut on the hill side covered in snow.

The northlooking hills frozen but visible;
The point on the circle where we pass
The early winter, warm, ageless.
Soon the moon bends a brown light
Over the salt marsh, the ashes of tamarisk.

Night faces the king's route west.
A millennium's waste of bronze and plastic
Litters the sea bed. You lie beyond
The terminal, brushed asleep by the restless,
Touching the moon with risen light.

AT HARDISTY'S FARM

for John and Hermione

One great Cause of Miscarriage in Men's affairs is that they too much regard the Present . . . But the Grand Mistake is that we know not w[t] *we mean by we or selves or mind etc.*

George Berkeley

I

There is a need for strangers;
The body needs them,
Desires not to know them,

Desires to be alone with them.
Their imposing necessity
Passes into us, survivors

Of the crowded mind who
Align window with window
And so avoid the house,

The black blood of the moor
Flaking from our shoes
As we casually descend;

Each man seeing the thing
He sees, seeing his neighbour
Committed to a certain illusion.

We too have come missing
The inexorable dictates
Of the cul-de-sac, in conversation

In disagreement, without a snood
Of loosened hair, together
Where the unreadable occurs:

The places we have not been know
Us well as border, definition.
The hills tilt daily

With the weight of our absence.
Lovers that never existed
In tales of the place come

Separately by inner roads
Where one is a standing friend
And another leads in silence.

II

I have an image curled
In the empty flasque of space,
The body of a violin,

Its original mould a weight
Of wood gradually abandoned,
Drilled to nothing, reduced

By a million strokes of the knife,
With its holes surviving
Merely as sound wrapped on

Coils of air, four axes
Which Hardisty never heard
Nor the troopers from the battle.

So there is nothing to give you
Save a book, a New Year's kiss,
Lost proofs; building

A small joke into my sombreness,
Making its voices for a moment
My voice speaking to you

And then in some humility
Abolishing that distinction.
To scrape the instrument entirely empty.

We live within each other and never touch;
No love is unrequited
Though locus amicus knows nothing

Of the "eternal rocks beneath",
Is a phrase delicate as belling fuschia,
As a bone redeemed, a trial-piece;

And the untenable house a place
Where the trees gather by virtue
Of our several loneliness.

III

The musicians have gone home;
The wall has been repaired.
Here by the mellow fire

We have paused to talk together,
After months now at ease,
Wishing the world upon our selves:—

The son's dream, falling
By the calendared wall
Till he reached a gable-

Window and entered;
The children's game, a ball
Sang and did not sing

In the air, bounded
By endless finite curves;
Bright objects

Of a man's energy and mind
Round on a former point
Which he never knows

For what the body has passed
May be conceiv'd
Annihilated. Obelus

In hand he punctures
History and space,
Releases nothing.

Let us instead remark
"How frost curtains
The smaller lights!"

For 'tis onely conceiving
A person affected
With those sensations.

"TO LAURA. . . ."

i

To smile is privacy
When the soft toil
Remits at night
So little casualty.

Love is the distance
Between display
And display,
A closure of all desire.

ii

To feel the dispensing of tea
A privilege, at least,
An order of words:
The historic target I set aside.

Nothing comes of nothing.
Yes, let us leave it at that.
I will mend my lights
And travel north, tomorrow.

iii

Who will fault
Your quiet presence
Among the nullities
I desert,

Apparitress,
Warm space,
Inhabited by
Achieved longing?

iv

Each year by retreating
We are more familiar
Till the difference
Grows to intimacy.

Such formality
Draws us together,
Endurance tender
As light years.

WINTER'S TALES

i

In declining dark
Our fixed expression took
The daily farm,
The cattle's frozen stook

From the urbane road.
What epiphenomena
Of the closed observer
Glistered our code?

With the same hour and
Differing light,
The house darkened the land,
Blotted the skyline.

ii

At sutured Towton
We came on a car
Its wheels splayed, only
Rescuable by abandon.

And there snow lay too;
The infinite verge
A white sheet bleaching
On a hedge;

Or, an abstract
Long, forgotten statue
Of the fallen,
Of the plough-hacked.

Now the house shone
With ancient lights
Though in slow approach
The driver had gone

From her immobile cell,
And through the snow
We met the fell
Droppings of an army.

iii

The sun fingers us,
And the mild collapse
Of our cold continuum
Unwraps the heroine.

With the springing earth
As pedestal
The unfixed eye
That pleases some, tries all.

How we have seen
Hermione stretched on Time;
And, feeding through quicklime,
The local fauna!

THE DEATH OF BOB STRACHAN

In foul January there was a moment
When the road dropping between
Intense firs and younger trees
Was stopped by a car.
No fear stood in the ditches.
The car, I am assured,
Was darker than bottlegreen,
And dust under the tyres
Sweet as a child's breath.
The obstacle so lately human
Birdsong had not resumed its chiselling.

Months after his Victorian mother
He stopped in winter
Between the wooden sides of the road,
Various bird- and- water-sounds,
The sun trembling
At the edge of the world.

PREVIOUSLY A PLACE

All this time we have stared at the house;
A skin of dry pink lime clasps the walls
Where the wall is high and blank, punctured
With a nine-light shield of cheap stained glass
Hung in retired splendour – but oddly
Outside, hanging over the echoing gateyard.

Nothing remarkable, but vacant
And available, with the good will
Thrown in, like the mannerly fuschia,
The stems peeling delicate blisters
Of wooden membrane, with scarlet and
Contaminated white bells in precipitation also.

At the other end the place departs
In embarrassment, under lowering
Roofs, wimpled iron not blue Bangor slates;
An awkward list of deponent relatives –
Scullery, back bedroom, appleroom,
Then the inhuman dairy, "chambers of maiden thought".

All afternoon we have considered
This endured survival: when we slammed
The doors of the car pausing to view,
A small volume of lime touched the path
Square and layered as a napkin and
Offered as it were just in case we felt ourselves at home.

MOUNT ARGUS

The grass rose in a mound
To a crest of white flaming seed;
The floss was white, and the truth is
Even then each shaking stem was white too.

The mass of it looked green
Or the shadow of each stem
On the million like it
Became green without reflection.

Branches of sycamore dipped
And dipped in the summer heat.
The blunt end of a mill house
Neatly appeared in the right corner.

So it was to the growing boy
Stirred by the plasma
Of water and rotten leaves
Trimming the field of his vision.

Now in the distant moment
It admits little of itself,
The fear of what he once knew,
The perfect, untouchable light.

"GREEN TO THE VERY DOOR"

For years
We had watched the illusion
High on the low side

Of the opposing valley,
Ellison's farm buildings,
A triangular arrangement

Of gable and drystone wall
With a long falling line
Of cupress meeting the road.

Nothing came between
Its perfect constituents:
The celtic brown

Of silent cattle
Browsing kneedeep
In barley and distance,

Or the soft bosom
Of dunghills
Warming the last

Wraiths of snow.
That was in the days
Of the Leclanché cell,

Shillings and pence et cetera,
Pence for the most part
That we uselessly hoarded.

Then a day came
Over many years
– We were elsewhere

And hardly noticed
How the drains simply
Burst with excrement

Refusing to split
Into our constructions.
We turned from each other

To look again at the
Vertical landscape.
I have been there now

Among the loud spaces:
I cannot step back
Across the air,

But stand in Ellison's parlour
Listening to my voice from
The eight corners of the room.

FOUR POEMS WITH THE SAME TITLE

NORTHERN CHAPEL I

We fought the rock with hinge and jamb
Who built this old Jerusalem;

Among such careless fields the heart
Found enemies in every art.

We grudged the wall its inch of grace
And windows shivered curtainless

That shades where present shadows sit
Be perpendicularly lit,

Pews here squarely face each other
Making each his neighbour's keeper.

And round the outside grave stones set
Artless as an alphabet.

NORTHERN CHAPEL II

Above the rectangular family stall, succeeding speakers addressed the features and blind necks (indifferently) of the generations, confronting forms that wept. Every one exhaled his neighbour across an argument of trodden soil. In their anticipated hell, ink exploded in its locket, and the air turned in arabesques of liquid mind. The pages beckoned with curling black fingers. Numbers marched through the walls.

NORTHERN CHAPEL III

Pale snow and mellow lichen
Cap the characters engraved;
Their lead convictions shrunken
Plummet the recent pavement.

Incurable fields renew
Rest-denying signs of rest.
Reader stumbles at the cross-
Roads, traveller at the word.

Salem was not built to last.
The heatless winter sun stalls
Aloft; expels a soft light
And lights our new expulsion.

NORTHERN CHAPEL IV

The church is empty at midnight, and within one hour none comes, or within a year. I propose two theses; Time changes all that cannot change: Order releases all that cannot move. I have come here, a lost familiar, with my irrational fears and meaningless responsibilities. And the place is altering: I am watching the whitewash by the noticeboard break down under the arclamp, a geology of pure moment, a sacrament of neglect.

LANDSCAPE WITH MINUTE WILDFLOWERS

The train moves
Stealthily along the shore
Denying its rails
Between inseparable sand
And stone. An invisible
Path leads under the cliff.

Never was green so close
To black, the waves
Pointless with motion,
Wind cranking itself
Through the sublime windows:
Nature is perpetual, alas.

Intent and purposeless,
Neither here nor there,
The process returns to me.
The wisp of diesel
Scaling the cliffs
Is a phrase of perfect execution.

Everything is discreet, nearly: -
The open church door
Of ten-league parishes
Clipped in the horizon,
Which beyond Downhill is
The straightest line in the world.

Viewed from the Mussenden
The sea was marble in the making:
Distant coasts
Curved into focus
Absorbed by liquid movements
And the cold fury of the place.

I stood high enough
To see the deep pools
Designing themselves,
Once when love seemed
At an end, and was not.
I return lowly, blind, at work too.

ON FAILING TO TRANSLATE

The rain had stopped maybe an hour ago.
We stood alone in the sodden garden
Waiting to go home or be driven
To some other furious hope.
Exhaust fumes lay at the bottom of the road
Grey upon grey, a carpet in a showroom.

Then I heard, suddenly as if it had started
To life, the rain still falling in the grass
Dropping between the blades and the leaves
With a motion which I knew must startle us.
And I said "This is love's benediction
And nothing more." The hands we held
Shaking in farewell were a bridge between
Us, pushing against either bank, a strength
Delicately equal to ours, but resisting always.

The water beneath us bubbled downwards
On its long journey back to the earth.

HOLLOW EDEN

Down by the cringing lawn
Hydrangeas net the air
And the interpreters
Have mapped a line to the south
So we fall within their care.

They have wired the bungalow
To another world while we slept;
Have taken away our childhood grammar,
And borrowed names from the garden
For their exchanges.

The murmur of intervening doors
Hides their direction,
And yet in this shared mood
Our hands flutter silently
At pelmet and counterpane.

They are urging us now
With their sweet logic
That nothing could be said
To improve the situation,
That nothing should be said.

We fall,
Miming the shape of prayers
In the arctic rooms
Where our grandparents died,
Simply well.

(How bitter the hills were then,
Where no gods presided,
Alternatively blue and golden,
Or dusty with spar and quartz.
- Amphitheatrical!)

Who have come together
Like swimmers shaking hands,
Hear the lifeguards
Toss and dream,
And do not hear each other.

SEVEN ACTIVE MEDITATIONS ON A DISTRICT OF NORTH CLARE

History does not repeat itself; yet
wherever something did not become
history and did not make history, then
history will by all means be repeated.
Ernst Bloch

1

Titania
Is not the spirit of the place.
She is
The light of the moonlined hills.

Visitor and presiding goddess
Soft-mouthed and spoken,
To tell by her
Tragedies do not occur:

The world at nightfall
Between the mountains and sea
Warbles like a small bird
And the simple outboard motor

Deceives no one.
Nature is a trade
In all seasons flourishing,
The whole thing short of a line.

2

In the same hills they call
    A spade a spade.
They know what's what:
    They have a word for it,

Pacified, hostile,
    Roosting on their wrists,
Birds of the same feather,
    Cock and crow.

*

A language less
    Tethered to my arm,
Eating a wider circle,
    Even the wrong

And succulent weeds
    We don't know
The names of.
    Speaking Utopian!

3

Houses in the place
    Brood on their cellars
Moving as though the last
    Pre-human giants

Whom time had not
    Left time to leave
Had caught in desolate flight
    Their windows and doors

Ablaze with light
    And chimneys full
With a downdraught of weeds.
    And the light breaks.

4

"How the door of the barracks is
    Empty as a tennis court
Though strangely upright
    And lacking a net!"

You smile. It is
    One of your wiles.
The analogy amuses
    Your strictly singular mind.

The years between us
    Unaccountable
Those we share
    As much a barrier.

The least substantial spaces
    Are roots of our being.
We are those we love
    And do not know.

5

East of Belle Harbour:-
    In the hour before sunfall
The picture envelops me
    As the sentence passes you by.

I take hope from you
    And recreate the site
The stiff carabiners
    Aiming to keep guard

Upright before correction
    Prisoners lolling
An instant on the walls
    Before death.

Such typical creations
    We never change!
Now under the dark hood
    Of a constant sky

Water never changes
    Colour from day to night
"The sun wet
    With recusant tears."

6

Today is continuously different
    And hearing Titania
(Impossible muse)
    To walk among the flags

We may speak
    Of thirty bone awkward
Souls cruising in childhood
    Off Newquay

They stood on water
    And the dealer
Who gave them soft burial
    Finds every wind a trade

Pillars the place
    And the oval sky behind
Turning the colour
    Of paper currency.

7

Never being here in winter
    When the sea melts the snow
And cattle are clubbed
    In the roofless yard

I preserve
    The grain of that door
The lie of its existence.
    What child you may ask

Slipped through its void
    This morning to play at soldiers
Or build a snowman
    Who is no pale imitation?

I try to know
    And by not being here
By being Titania
    Your visitor and lover.

Basking at Easter
    We heard shots
Fired across the blue grave
    Neither towards and never away.

We were old children
    With one conceit left
– These words breaking like
    White heads of the sea.

II

FIGURE WITHOUT LANDSCAPE

The dark rope I drag behind me
    Is my long companion.
A beast on the road to market
    Has lost her master.
I find fear among the women,
    Hatred and lust in the men.
They turn their shoulders
    Who flattered the broad of my back.
They wail of love
    Looking out at me.

This place that knows me
    Is no place for the sweet note.
I make confession
    In the next parish.
(It was a bad year, father.
    Would-be foster mothers
Thought they might not be paid,
    Fearing the French invasion.)

The few are placed in
    A household with cows.
They mostly die,
    It cannot well be otherwise.
Gathering wayside dung,
    Invisible to historians
Yet transparently honest:-
    Their outsides looking
Like their insides.
    One it was said
"More resembled a liver
    Than any human thing."

The solitary bump
    On the belly of the lawn
In sight of the flashing windows,
    The lurid and tall door.
Dead or deserted:
    It did not matter.
Mine did not die from attack
    By water-rats or pigs.
You can keep your bad cess:
    I have seen your lost demesnes,
Heard the fluent rivers
    Babble a' green fields.
But from these moving times,
    I cannot touch your slender
Adjectival life.
    In August I open headlands
A sickle asking questions
    Above my head.
Ruth without Boaz –
    Premature in that too.

DIARIST I

January:
    fine, frosty weather this month.
Farmers putting out manure
    from headlands.
At the fuller's mill I saw
    an otter fishing.

Wet half the day now.
    Not a native tree green
Except the holly, some furze
    and the red laurel.
The oats have failed that were
    broadcast at Michaelmas.

Heavy rains, floods;
    a bog moving in Ulster
Owing to water under it;
    cattle being swept away.
Tense the sequence of months;
    all's blistered, rugate.

April, "dripping, bleating, new".
    Yellowblue stalks
Broken in the field.
    Livid mouths
Swollen with hunger.
    18/- a barrel for oats.

Fierce fighting near Warsaw;
    the papers speak little

Of Callan's poor,
    fifteen hundred souls
In anguish.
    The twenty sixth day,

Saint Stephen's:
    a fine, thinclouded
Calm day with some sun.
    Soldiers and country boys
Scuffled
    on Thursday,

A frosty, bright sunny morning,
    ice on pools,
Day's end freshcold, sharp;
    the beginning of night
Moonlit, then covered with cloud.
    I live increasingly

On paper.
    Patrick Doran gaoled
For his part
    against the soldiers.
A heavyclouded morning;
    day's end foggish.

DIARIST II

Aghast this morning, looking from the yard
Over the near mist and balmy granite
Of our new chapel, aghast to find the

Long continuity of hedge and ditch,
Endless and various means of maintaining
The green rows which hold the fields together,

The corners cut not a moment too soon,
The gaps and gates swallowed in energy
Though conscious with birdsong buried in growth.

And then turn to this empty ledger!
The sloping desk and the worn initials
Of pre-Emancipation,

to find the gully
Of my nib dried up or the inkpot burst
With the night's frost.

Is it bitterness or
Grace drives me to it, to an endeavour
Where perfection is at best avoided?

THE PROCESS

(for Dennis and Sylvia Tate)

I was sitting
on a high stool in Gort
watching the empty square

between the streets.
There is no square
at the centre,

just the abutment
of four incomplete
streets on nothing.

A donkey and cart
slumbered by the ruins
of a rusting Morris *Minor*

— the boot flourishing
with dry grass.
The animal was prone

as wood; the creels
tense with muscular
exhaustion.

Nobody moved near me
in the renovated hall
though two farmers lounged

on slender glasses
half-full of stout,
by the still piano.

*

Then the fire siren
broke into the square
slamming the door

by the honeysuckle;
a red invisible bull
or other image.

Like any traveller
of bright modesty
I stood in respect.

The donkey and cart
rose and jockeyed
towards one street

while noise circled
with black pages
of the querist overhead.

Fire siren filled
the empty town of Gort,
and no man moved

from the shadow of doors
for the light still held
its fifty-year-old

pot-still weak potency.
Those who were about me
did not falter.

*

I had forgotten
their deep arcana,
forgotten too

the burden of the donkey,
the agony of his avocation.
The engine in the chassis'

loins dropped the depth
of rust towards the ground.
The speakers parted

on a paradox,
their tumblers lined
with drying air.

"There's no use me
reading the newspapers.
There's only in them

things that I don't know."
In southern Cloyne,
over unapproved roads

and air shining
like a box of knives,
a bishop's shade relaxed.

Entirely I forgot
the siren, firing
Coole with my enthusiasm.

UNDER THE WALLS

The hall was a bolus
Of ultramarine
And the ridiculous vase
Smaller and deeper still.
Chairs led downwards
To the chess boards.

We gathered
By the incapacitated
And their matron.
The discussion
Cleared much away
And moved in us love
Of the present,
Of handskill and action,
Who are impatient,
Who have not stilled
The historical voice,
The carbon words that neither
Cut nor break.

Prick-faced, brutal
We turned to leave,
Volunteers to fate;
But the doorway fluttered
With distant leaves and petals,
And steeplestones grew
Through the ruined choirs
Upwards, sapping the sky,
Never tired.

And so our eyes detained us.
By the burning door
A manor owl stood
On polished claws,
Its body solid
As a bole of timber yet
Absorbed with movement,
Bleeding to the floor,
Claws nibbing
The immediate children.

Where we are needed
We rest;
Our voices draw
The innocent and lean together.
In the ancient country
They call us tricoteuses
Who are less
That gentle patients,
Lost in a weather
That we cannot lose.

Our hope is not
To change the future –
A red invisible
Bull burying
His horns in the ground!
(There is no word for peace
Until the trooper counts
His loss before he kills,
The orphan finds his mother
Before he cries.)

We live in history
And have no moral language:
Trees that are spoken
Have betrayed us.

But the stuffed bird
In the conservatory,
The forty-year-old widow
On the scrubbed doorstep
Remain to move.
We are in pain
With them, living.

We are yesterday
Totally transformed, the
Uncertainty of last year,
The serenity of
Sixteen forty one.
There is no mirror
In the forest;
That day succeeds night
Is merely a figure of speech.

QUINTA DEL SORDO

in memory of Michael Devereux
disappeared in the winter of 1940/1,
and George Plant who died 5/3/1942.

A flat light
    came over the sheds
to spill down
    the galvanised roof

when tar began to
    shine towards midday
and the roofs dipped in salute
    or levelled

like our children's guns.
    This was the present then
a thatched house
    ironically renewed

dense yellow solidness
    boxed between the housewall
open shed and the
    diaphragm of the gate.

*

The fields moved
    on several planes
a planetarium
    flexible deluding

among raised ditches
    a geometer's nightmare.
As buttons of tar popped
    on the desolate roofs

the kitchen drew in its breath
    behind the dark window
and Grandfather Goya
    in the alcove shook his brush

(There follows
    a brief sentence describing
Devereux's body,
    the dismantled car concealed

in dunghills through the county,
    and Plant's ultimate conviction
on revoked evidence.
    Quinta del Sordo.)

"There are no natural lines
    only mass, reflection
and the energy of the eye."
    Through ribs of the alder

light heroically
    bared the sky.
It was foolish, vacuous
    touched with moments

of subdued pity
    disproportionate to the sight.
So long, ago
    so still

the land lay
    like a great cunt
smiling with its usual
    poetic convenience

and several swallows
    had the goodness
to make dummy runs
    at earth's virtue.

* * *

Nothing remains
    of virtue and atrocity;
fur and the nail's breadth
    of Man and the Quadrumana

"answering"
    to the claw and hoof of
other animals and birds
    briefly flourish.

The grave or cave is no-one's,
    who bury purely in time.
Nothing remains
    unmoved, the elements

continually release
    the mind they fashion.
Receding in
    contained lucidity

the tyre tracks
    melt in spring's mud;
the meadows
    obey, ignore us.

III

FROM THE GERMAN OF JOHANNES BOBROWSKI

FOR MARIA SIPICZKY

TO KLOPSTOCK

If I did not want the active whole:
this, I say
river and wood
but have into my sense
bound the darkness,
voice of the hastening bird, the arrow-
shaft of light around the slope

and the sounding waters -
how should I
speak your name
(if any fame
were mine): I have
preserved what I passed,
shadefable of complicity
and of atonement:
so as I trust
acts - you mastered that -
I trust also
the language of the forgetful.
Flightless,
down into the winters,
I speak out of a reed,
their word.

TO BE NAMED, ALWAYS

To be named, always:
the tree, the bird in flight,
the reddish rock, where the river
pulls, green, and the fish
in white smoke, when it darkens
down over the woods.

Signs, colours, it is
a game, I am thoughtful,
it might not end
a-right.

And who is to teach me
what I forgot: the stones'
sleep, sleep
of the birds in flight, the trees'
sleep, in the dark
does their utterance go on?

Were a god there
and in flesh,
and able to call me, I would
walk about, I would
wait a little.

THE DON

High, out of fires
the villages. Above the rock
the banks fall. But
the river caught, icebreath
it blew, stillness darkly
followed after it.

White was the river. The higher
bank dark. The horses
climbed up the slope. Once,
the banks beyond
flew away, we saw
behind the fields distant
under the early moon walls
against the sky.

There
the Diva sings,
in the tower,
he cries to the cloud - the bird
of utter pain, he calls
over the rockbanks,
commands the plains to hear.
O hills, open yourselves, he says,
step forth armed;
(to the dead), put on your helmets.

LIGHTING BACK

Twilight.
How the grassland
moves here, the wide current,
plains. Cold, untimely
the moon. A wingbeat now.

On the banks of rivers,
distant,
when the broad
sky held them embraced,
we heard singing
in the woodshade. The ancestor
searched for overgrown ditches.

Birdheart, light, feathered
stone on the wind.
Falling
into the mists. Grass and the earth
receive you, for a death
moment, a snail's track.

But
who is to bear me,
man with closed eyes,
evil-mouthed, hands
that hold nothing, who follows
the river, dying of thirst,
who in the rains
breathes the other age,
which comes no more, other and
unspoken, like clouds,
a bird with open wings,
raging, against the sky,
a counterlight, wild.

VILLAGE CHURCH 1942

Smoke
on snowroof and beamwall.
Over the drop
down crowtracks. But the river
in ice.

There
snowglare, shattered
stone, masonry, the arch,
broken the wall,

where the village stood
against the hill, the river
sprang in early year,
a lamb, before the door,
a round harbour
was for the wind,

which goes through
the heights, dark, its own
shadow, it calls, harshly

the crow
screams back to it.

MEMORIAL

Years,
gossamer,
the great spiders, years -
the gipsies travelled
the clay path with horses. The old gipsy chief

came with the whip, the women
stood in the gateyard, talking
in crooked arms
the handful of happiness.

Later they were not seen.
Then came the killers with leaden
eyes. Once, the old woman
above in the loft
asked about the missing.

Hear the rain streaming
down the slope, they are moving,
who no-one else can see,
on the old clay path,
enveloped in spray,
foreign crowns of wind
over their black hair,
lightly.

IV

He made darkness his secret place;
His pavilion round about him
Were dark waters and thick clouds of the skies.

SURVIVORS OF PAVILION

"Soldier, there is a war between the mind
And sky, between thought and day and night. It is
For that the poet is always in the sun,

Patches the moon together in his room
To his Virgilian cadences, up down,
Up down. It is a war that never ends.

Yet it depends on yours."

Wallace Stevens

i

Nights before, sleep spiked the gods.
Her eyes circled like targets;
his cheeks suddenly fawned, puffed.
The mixed blessing of childhood:
two broken speeches – Mother

Irish strained beyond risk of
loveliness; Father laboured
to make his first thousand. Failed.
Toys cuddled me that foreseen
night. I die too, lose magic.

ii

This is the month's mind, a gap
in the body when the soul
should rest. But Lent was loving -
time as Swift once proved groaning
with semen against the lap

of dreamgirls stuck to his bed.
"Papist Ireland romped like fish
in what was wine." And moving
at your corded side I wish
for better doubts – have you bled?

iii

Sleep stumbles to the green door
of waking, it curtains sway.
Fearing the jury of dreams
we light braziers against day;
shadows swim across the floor

in our beached cottage. The seams
of cracked lino like the sea
roar this one sentence " will the
drunken eighteenth-century
judges come for us tonight?"

iv

Empty and light against clouds
each tree stands an inch beyond
its eastern filament. Sedge-
like snow sends out its fronds;
the air warms gradually

with these winter images.
While the familiar green nods
for their passion to abate . . .
we begin to move, tree and
spectre come even closer.

v

Here somethings happen but not
necessarily begin.
Remember the ochre inns
on jig-saw puzzles; horses
tired to bits wait for a start.

The ground foxes where the sun
falls, and shade kisses the stain;
the paper is yesterdays.
But a man steps to the light
with eyes for the washed mountain.

vi

Who are you you asked. Answer
yourself for none knows better.
They make us bad at being
bad. You turn your hard Dresden
face, and below it blood lurks.

And a kiss you give me when
I visit your pink clinic,
its brick subdued from young red;
like your silent mouth for it
is clean and lustreless, bled.

I lie between two battles,
yours and ours, the engagements
meaningless now and falling
into a seamless future.
Utterable privacy.

vii

A pierhead is their globe where
in the paint the sea becomes
a quilt of colour; light ebbs
on the sill of far islands
glowing rare as ebony.

Their smack is stitched to the tide.
Like a wrecked sea the pier swims
in viscid oil. The flags burn
under their feet when they land
like fishes, gasp at the play.

viii

If the hill's a flight of steps
it leads to the lichened sky.
He is sitting on the well
and the white horse is lapping
him, half way to the castle.

There is no night; he is breaking in sleep. The castle is
dimly lit and the sky aches.
Water is flowing from his
sides; his cupped hands are empty.

ix

One day to the last day comes
again. Weary with newness
we resign in the warm blast

of a distant occurrence.
Let us mistake it for drums,

hear on the cold volcano
dance percussion, the air-rush
of carnival atmosphere.
Then in a permanent glimpse
trap the passacaglia.

But the first sign was pressure
at the window and the thud
of smoke. We were rushing through
the plantation and fearful
of what we might ask ourselves.

How different from Stubbs' cream
ponies who pull their basket
in woodlands devoid of air.
There no dance begins, nor does
the temperature ever change.

x

The emblem is made of jaws.
(Closed it held a torch aloft.)
In a night of running skies
it snaps open with a sigh
like a pair of dividers.

Ironmongers mending the lamp
scarcely have time to notice
a girl's six-inch breasts, levelled
like pistols because of her
stomach which is full of blood.

As she imagines what soft
explosions they could have made
in her sweet, addled lake (oil
boiling in her clothes) the lamp
sunders with a squeal of flesh.

Food stores run out; a whole pig
floats away out of vision,
its throat cut like a red slice
of pineapple. The bridge brims
with water moving like skin.

xi

In the wood of self-killers
trunks writhe: in particular
one with leaves blonde as tinder.
Slack skin crackles and her head
is slumped between her dry breasts.

Memory urges the lips up,
A pool of sky opens and
we see clouds but no matter.
Squad cars police the nurseries;
the glass houses are barren.

Outside the morning patrol
pauses, two youths from Bradford
– shorthaired hooligans to some –
and a mulatto playing
bongos on his rifle-butt.

Throw back the curtains and pray
this is unreality
outside? There is no distance
between my head and his head.
I see a stone wrapped in skin.

A street is two parallel
desolations. From habit
of the warm world men still walk
the road between two nothings
imagining houses, lives.

xii

Enter by the metal fates.
Cold laurels close round your head.
White hearts bubble beneath ice;
a gull stands on feet and beak
waiting to stab at the thread.

The three figures in bronze wait
after war through our winter,
two standing still as always.
Clotho at the rere supports
a ball of twine passing it

across her companions' breasts.
In a free hand Lachesis
displays a sprig of olive
while in front of them the last
Fate sits dropping the taper

onto a brown film of ice:
Atropos stares straight ahead.
None of the women has seen
a length of stiffened bronze thread
slip from the composition.

These gentle and arrogant
dwellers in the iron field
put forth their cold aureoles.
Whatever the care they wheeled
they pavilion worst want.

A NOTE

Irish poets, like Jewish mothers, are often taken as representative of their race. I should prefer to speak of their avocations – poetry and motherhood – which are at once universal and immediate. Race, by comparison, is a *chimera.*

A variety of readers react promptly to allusions of a political or historical kind. Some indulge a topographical sentiment and attachment; others resist any specification of a cultural tradition not their own. The one reaction is as limiting as the other. To all readers I offer the observation that when one encounters a signpost reading New Bliss, one is elsewhere.

The comments on particular poems which follow are intended to dispel imtimacy as much as resistance, for these attitudes are opposite sides of the same unilinear reading of poetry. They are suggestions, rather than comprehensive annotations.

Eblana. A site marked on Ptolemy's map of the known world identified with the location of Dublin. Here, Eblana is city, woman, and muse.

Beaumaris. A faded holiday resort in Anglesey, North Wales, dominated by an unfinished, and therefore undamaged, castle.

At Hardisty's Farm. Like *Winter's Tales* and *Four Poems* this poem relates to the landscape of West Yorkshire.

"To Laura . . . " Petrarch's.

Landscape with Minute Wildflowers. At Downhill in County Derry, Frederick Hervey, earl of Bristol and bishop of Derry, built a large house: a neo-classical temple on the cliff top commemorates his cousin Mrs. Mussenden.

Figure Without Landscape. See Kenneth Connell's essay on illegitimacy in *Irish Peasant Society* from which I quote the phrase in inverted commas.

Diarist I. In part a translation/summary of passages from Humphrey O'Sullivan's diary: see Irish Text Society edition.

The Process. Zealots in Philadelphia will know all too well that Lady Gregory's house at Coole was not burned, though such things are permitted to happen in poems. Indeed poems have that responsibility.

Under the Walls. Written following a visit to an eighteenth-century house in County Meath mistaken for Coolamber Manor. The house has been converted into a home fór disabled children. 1641 was of course particularly disturbed in Ireland by events which had their repercussions in the English Civil War.

Quinta del Sordo. "Deafman's House", the name of Goya's house. The events summarised in the dedication occurred in the context of an internal IRA dispute.

From the German of Johannes Bobrowski.
Bobrowski was born at Tilsit, East Prussia, in 1917; intending to study art, he was conscripted in 1939, and at the end of the war he opted to live in the German Democratic Republic. His concern in poetry was to bring from his obsession with the past "ne that stays news". He died in East Berlin in September 1965.

Survivors of Pavilion. Written between 1970 and 1980, with many additions and subtractions considered before the present poem was completed, primarily in or about Ulster. *Not* studies in private and public suffering but based on the publicity art forces us to suffer in, the isolation such a politics instils. There are glimpses of Jack Yeats paintings in v, vii and viii; a vestige of Dante in xi; the sculpture described in xii is located at the south eastern gate of Saint Stephen's Green, Dublin, presented to the people of Ireland by the people of West Germany in acknowlegment of aid at the end of the Second World War.

Personally I think the dominant concern of this collection is the tragedy of premature revolution; politically, I consider the poems metaphysical notations of answerable poignancy.